I would like to dedicate this book to the person reading it right now. You have supported and encouraged me on my journey, and I am so grateful for you. I want this book to inspire you and motivate you to keep going. I want you to remember how loved and valuable you are. I want you to challenge yourself to become the best *you* that you can be!

—MF

DISCLAIMER: This book is written as a source of information only. The information contained herein should by no means be considered a substitute for the advice of a qualified medical professional, who should always be consulted before beginning any new diet, exercise, or other health program. The reader is responsible for checking the ingredients before using the recipes in this book to determine if any ingredient may cause an allergic or other adverse reaction. All efforts have been made to ensure the accuracy of the information contained in this book as of the date published. The author and publisher expressly disclaim responsibility for any adverse effects arising from the use or application of the information contained herein. All product names and trademarks are the property of their respective owners, which are in no way associated or affiliated with Little Bee Books, Inc. Product names are used solely for the purpose of identifying specific products. Use of these names does not imply any cooperation or endorsement.

BuzzPop
an imprint of Little Bee Books
251 Park Avenue South, New York, NY 10010
Copyright © 2020 by Paws On Media, LLC
All rights reserved, including the right of reproduction in whole or in part in any form.
BuzzPop and associated colophon are trademarks of Little Bee Books.
Author photo by Andre Nguyen © 2020

Manufactured in China TPL 0620
First Edition

1 3 5 7 9 10 8 6 4 2
ISBN 978-1-4998-1030-1

buzzpopbooks.com

For more information about special discounts on bulk purchases,
please contact Little Bee Books at sales@littlebeebooks.com.

THIS BOOK BELONGS TO

....

FAVORITE TREAT

....

BEST DANCE MOVE

....

DREAM TALENT

....

I WILL USE THIS BOOK TO BECOME

....

....

TABLE OF CONTENTS

Introduction 6

Mind 8

Body 32

Spirit 56

My Final Musings 92

Acknowledgments 95

About the Author 96

INTRODUCTION

Hey, I'm Meredith Foster! Many of you know that I created my YouTube channel in 2009 and originally named it STILABABE09. As I shared my passions and personality with the world, I slowly gained an audience who became a community of young women all wanting to see one another flourish. In response, I started sharing more and more of my life, and ventured into vlogging as well, taking my audience on a more personal journey with me.

I talk a lot about how important it is to stay positive, have confidence, and embrace everything that makes you YOU. But guess what? It's one thing to talk about how important it is to stay true to yourself, and another thing to actually DO it. Trust me, I know how hard it can be! We're constantly facing messages and images from the media, from friends online, and from negative people in our lives who aim to tear us down and make it even more difficult to celebrate our true, beautiful selves.

That's why I want to put a little good out into the world with this book and help you find ways to maintain positivity, find your motivation, and feel comfortable in your own skin. Here, you'll get an inside look on what was happening behind the camera for me all these years. I open up about my struggles and how I dealt with growing up in the age of social media. You'll also learn the history of my relationship with myself, my body, and my friends, and read along with years' worth of poetry that I wrote when I was at my lowest before finding my faith and purpose for living again. I hope you'll be inspired by this book and its activities inside. If I'm asking you to take on the challenges of this journey, it's only fair I share my own struggles—and successes!

This book is broken into Mind, Body, and Spirit because we should make sure we're paying attention to *all three* key parts of ourselves! It can be easy to place all your focus on one and end up totally ignoring the other two. But we all need a strong mind, strong body, AND strong spirit to start being truly happy and healthy!

Thank you for reading my book and sharing my journey. Now let's get to fostering our best selves!

Before you dive into each section, let's do a quick little check-in.

5 WAYS TO START FEELING GOOD NOW!

For each item on the list, circle a number from 1 to 3 to rate where you are right now. Don't worry, this isn't a test! It's to help YOU only. When you're done, you'll see what areas you're already great at and be able to consider how you'll reach your next milestone.

 I struggle with this. 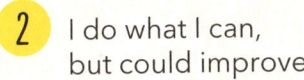 I do what I can, but could improve. 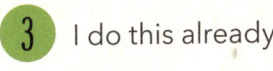 I do this already.

Drink water every morning before you eat your first meal. (It helps get your organs and digestive system working!)

Avoid doing these things: trying to please everyone, fearing change, living in the past, overthinking, being afraid to be different, sacrificing your happiness for others, thinking you're not good enough, thinking you don't have a purpose.

Volunteer in your community. Giving back is so important!

Move your body! Moving around for 30 minutes a day can release endorphins! These endorphins interact with the receptors in your brain to reduce your perception of pain. Regular exercise has been proven to reduce stress, boost self-esteem, and improve sleep.

Spend more time outside, in nature, and off your phone.

Now that you've done your check-in, find the motivation that matches the most numbers you picked!

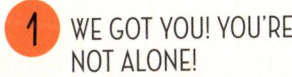 WE GOT YOU! YOU'RE NOT ALONE! 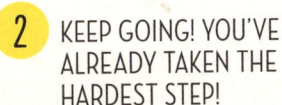 KEEP GOING! YOU'VE ALREADY TAKEN THE HARDEST STEP!  HIGH FIVE FOR YOU!

MIND

MIND OVER MATTER

You are always enough. The moment you have to prove your worth is when you walk away.

What was a negative thought that drifted through your mind today? Write it down here.

....
....
....

Then tear out this page, rip it up, and throw it away!

Now replace that negativity with a positive thought you'd prefer to have instead. Write it down here. Repeat this thought in your head every morning when you first wake up. Watch your perspective shift!

MISTAKES MAKE THE WOMAN

Eventually, the rose-colored glasses fell off and the truth was revealed. We believed the lie for so long, the truth was hard to swallow. When we did, we were set free.

We all make the wrong decision sometimes, and we don't always realize it until some time has passed. Think back to mistakes you've made or regrets you have. Then consider the lessons you've learned from those choices, and how they've made you who you are right now!

MISTAKE: ....
....
....
....
....

LESSON: ....
....
....
....
....

ME, MYSELF, AND I

A healthy relationship with yourself will lead to healthy relationships with others. But that doesn't come automatically—you've gotta put some time in for yourself, just like you would for anything else in your life! Here's how I indulge in me time: hot tea, playing the piano, warm baths, yoga, walks in nature, and baking!

Write down 1 thing you will do each day for a week that will nourish your relationship with yourself.

She treated herself the way she wanted her soul to be treated: with tenderness and care.

MONDAY: ....

....

TUESDAY: ....

....

WEDNESDAY: ....

....

THURSDAY: ....

....

FRIDAY: ....

....

SATURDAY: ....

....

SUNDAY: ....

....

QUIZ: WHAT KIND OF BOOK SHOULD YOU READ NEXT?

Sometimes, it can help to turn your mind off and get lost in someone else's for a while. Spend some time with a great book! But what kind of book is calling your name? Take this quiz to find out!

When you read or hear a story, you want to:

    A. Piece together clues to discover the big reveal

    B. Get a happily ever after

    C. Be totally transported to a new place

    D. Feel what it's like to be someone else

What TV shows are you obsessed with?

    A. True crime documentaries like *Making a Murderer*

    B. Dishy stories like *Riverdale*

    C. Epic tales like *Game of Thrones*

    D. Character-driven dramas like *This Is Us*

Your bags are packed and a plane is waiting to take you anywhere in the world. Where do you go?

    A. London

    B. Paris

    C. Hogwarts (Hey, I did say anywhere!)

    D. New York City

You're at a school dance with all of your friends and notice a cute new student you've never seen before standing off to the side, alone. Your first thought is:

A. I'll have to question my classmates to find out what everyone knows about this newcomer.

B. How can I arrange our perfect meet-cute moment?!

C. It's times like this I really need mind-reading powers.

D. I love meeting new people! I want to go strike up a conversation.

Which sentence is most intriguing to you?

A. She had been truly enjoying herself until the body was discovered in the coat closet.

B. Her heart pounded after she pressed SEND, and she stared at her screen for what felt like an eternity to await his reply.

C. The dragon carriages weren't usually her chosen method of transportation, but at this point, she'd do anything to get to the castle fast enough.

D. I knew I had to tell my mom how I felt then and there, or else I'd never have the chance to again.

RESULTS

MOSTLY As - MYSTERY
Whether it's a modern thriller or a good, old-fashioned British detective story, a mystery is sure to bring on the action and suspense you're craving!

MOSTLY Bs - ROMANCE
Who doesn't *love* love? A sweet and satisfying romance will give you all the good feels.

MOSTLY Cs - FANTASY
Nothing is a better escape than a story set in a fantastical world that doesn't even exist . . . or *does* it?

MOSTLY Ds - MEMOIR
Everyone has a story worth telling. Memoirs that reveal deeply personal, touching, or challenging moments from another person's life are just the medicine you need.

I GOT MOSTLY Cs! I love anything fantasy. I love being brought into a totally new world and immersing myself in it for a few hours.

VISION FOR THE FUTURE

She dreamed of a world filled with color. The desires of her heart were pure love that she wished to spread to every soul she met.

Let's make a vision board! You will need:

- Old magazines
- Glue or tape
- Scissors
- A sheet of paperboard

Think about goals you have for your future. They can be related to school, a hobby, your dream career—anything! Come up with 5 goals and then find images in the magazines to represent each one on your vision board. Cut out the images and attach them to the paperboard with tape or glue. Hang the completed vision board in your room and look at it every day to keep you inspired!

MY GOALS FOR THE FUTURE

1. ....
2. ....
3. ....
4. ....
5. ....

ALL-YEAR RESOLUTION

Who says January 1st is the only day you can set resolutions for yourself? I think it's good to give yourself a fresh start and try new things all year round! Answer these questions to help you come up with some resolution ideas.

WHAT'S SOMETHING THAT'S BEEN ON YOUR BUCKET LIST FOR YEARS?

....
....
....

WHAT WOULD YOU DO IF YOU COULD OVERCOME YOUR FEAR?

....
....
....

WHAT MAKES YOU RIDICULOUSLY HAPPY?

....
....
....

WHAT'S A BAD HABIT YOU'VE BEEN MEANING TO BREAK?

....
....
....

Think about your answers and use them to come up with one AWESOME resolution for yourself. Aim high, but make it realistic. Write it here—your resolution starts NOW!

....

....

....

....

....

....

....

....

....

....

....

....

CLEARING OUT THE CLUTTER

I don't know about you, but organizing and clearing out the messy spaces around me helps me clear my mind, too. Here's a list of ideas on how you can get started on some spring cleaning (or anytime-of-the-year cleaning!). Check off the ones you'd like to tackle, and then make your own personalized to-do list on the next page, including any ideas of your own. Just wait and see how accomplished you'll feel after completing even one of these tasks!

- [ ] Go through *everything* hanging in your closet and donate what you don't wear anymore (be honest!).

- [ ] Clean out your desk drawers and recycle all those old papers, birthday cards, and receipts that have piled up over the years.

- [ ] Take a serious look at your makeup collection and toss anything that might be expired or outdated. (Looking at you, roll-on body glitter from fifth grade!)

- [ ] When was the last time you got rid of old socks and underwear? (Maybe never?!) Time to say goodbye to anything with holes!

- [ ] Are there any books on your shelf just gathering dust? They'd look a lot better at a local used bookstore or library, where another reader can enjoy them!

- [ ] Virtual de-cluttering counts, too! Go through old files saved on your computer or cloud account and delete what you don't need anymore. Then organize what's left into handy folders so you can find things easily in the future.

My De-Cluttering To-Do List

CALENDAR

Take a look back at the last few pages. You've set goals, made resolutions, and planned to take time for yourself and your space—*phew!* Now, take a moment to get everything organized. This calendar is for you to take all those amazing ideas and plan out how you can make them happen! Don't freak out—you don't have to do everything at once. This is just to get you started thinking about the baby steps you'll take to make all of your dreams a reality. Try setting different goals for each week to make sure you're always aiming high!

Just as the sun rises every morning,
the sun sets into the horizon;
each day brings a chance to be brand-new.

SUNDAY	MONDAY	TUESDAY	WEDNESDAY	THURSDAY	FRIDAY	SATURDAY

DREAM JOURNAL

When we're asleep, our minds are finally free to go in any direction they choose. We dream every single night whether we realize it or not! Our dreams can reveal hopes, fears, and even creative ideas! They can also provide guidance for a current situation if you seek to interpret the dream you had. Right when I started dieting and denying myself certain foods, I had a dream that I was sitting on a couch eating Ben & Jerry's ice cream straight out of the pint! (Which was something I used to do as a kid.) I remember in the dream, I felt really guilty about it. Years later, I experienced that same feeling in real life. I was actually afraid of ice cream because I thought it would cause me to gain weight. I think this dream was highlighting what I was fearful of and trying to get me to recognize it before the unnecessary fear consumed my life. Looking back, I wish I could tell myself how worthy I am of these foods. YOU are worthy, too!

For one week, try dream journaling! Write down any dreams you have—even if you can't remember all the details or the full story—as soon as you wake up. If you find yourself not remembering ANY dreams, write about whatever is on your mind when you first wake up in the morning. That may be just as revealing!

Monday:

Tuesday:

Wednesday:

Thursday:

Friday:

Saturday:

Sunday:

....
....
....
....
....
....
....
....
....
....
....

Look back at your dreams and early morning thoughts from the past week. What stands out to you? Do you notice any patterns? What do you think your dreams are trying to tell you?

....
....
....
....
....

BODY

DIETING = RECIPE FOR DISASTER

Dieting makes you believe that if you just get small enough, you'll finally be worthy to take up space. Take up space, make those gainz, baby! I tried the keto diet and completely cut out entire food groups that my body needed! I was tired all the time and couldn't get a good night's sleep. I tried intermittent fasting and just felt hangry all the time. Learning to eat intuitively can be challenging when you've been raised on diet culture your whole life. Stop telling yourself that your "life will be better" once you look a certain way. It won't. One of my favorite quotes is by Esther Hicks: "The reason you want every single thing that you want, is because you think that you will feel really good when you get there. But, if you don't feel good on your way to there, you can't get there. You have to be satisfied with what-is while you're reaching for more." Life is already happening NOW! You are not a number on a scale, a size, or a look. Happiness is not having abs and lean legs. We can get so focused on what our bodies look like that we forget what truly matters!

What diets have you tried in the past? How did your body feel while you were following each one? How did you feel *inside*? Take a moment to reflect and fill in the table in the next page.

I ate/I did NOT eat . . .	Physically, I felt . . .	Emotionally, I felt . . .

Developing a healthy relationship between yourself and food may not happen overnight. Use baby steps to get there. Never feel shame or guilt about what you may be struggling with. We are ALL works in progress. What counts is that you acknowledge where you are and are honest with yourself and God. What has helped me in my journey was opening up to people I could trust and really leaning on God's word. I prayed and listened to worship music anytime I started having disorganized thoughts. Telling a trusted adult or friend that you are struggling is one of the best ways to start healing. Being vulnerable and open about where you are is how you create a connection that helps this healing. This was the turning point for me on my journey. Don't let fear stop you. Do not partner with the lies in your head. Fear wants to stop you from being your true self! You were created to live free!

FEELINGS ABOUT FOOD

I used to feel extreme guilt about eating certain foods I deemed "unhealthy." When you tell yourself you can't have a certain food, your body will only crave it more. Having that ice cream or treat you've been denying yourself becomes all you can think about.

For a minute, ignore ANY worries you may have about your body, your weight, or what is healthy vs. unhealthy. What are the top 3 foods that you absolutely can't live without? I know what mine are!

1. ....
2. ....
3. ....

Don't deny yourself those amazing foods! When I crave a cookie, I will just eat one (or a few, heh, heh) and move on with my day. Instead of ignoring my body, I listen to what it wants.

My Foodie Faves

Here are my top three foods!

- Chocolate (in any form!)
- Something crunchy & salty
- Peanut Butter

MOM'S HEALTHY CHOCOLATE CHIP COOKIES

If you watch my vlogs, you know I love my cookies. I have a major sweet tooth! So when I want a treat that's a little healthier, I will make my mom's famous "healthy" cookies! I love this recipe because it's so easy to remember. I usually just make it off the top of my head.

Serves: 3-4 people

    2 ripe bananas, mashed

    1 cup oats

    1 tsp coconut oil

    1 tsp baking soda

    handful of chocolate chips

    dash of cinnamon

    dash of nutmeg

Optional add-ins:

    walnuts

    coconut flakes

Mix all ingredients together and form into balls. Place on a cookie sheet lined with parchment paper. Bake at 350 degrees for 10-12 minutes. Set aside to cool.

BODY IMAGE

A positive body image is something I feel very passionately about. I've always loved the saying from Kahlil Gibran, "beauty is a light in the heart." It couldn't be more true! We are so much more than outer appearances. We need to redefine beauty in ways that are better for our health. Your body at its healthiest might not look the way you wish it did, and that "perfect body" image you have in your mind might only be achieved through unhealthy actions.

I'm speaking from experience. I got lip injections because someone told me I'd look better with big lips. The injections were not only super-painful, but also embarrassing because they made me look like a puffer fish. I spent hours crying while looking at myself in the mirror. I had done this to try to fit that "perfect" image others had placed in my head instead of embracing the beautiful features God gave me.

Our outside does not define our worth and it does not define our health, either! Beauty is not skin-deep; it is a light that shines out from the heart and onto others.

Let's start setting goals that are focused on how you FEEL inside your body, and what you can do rather than how you look. This is a powerful way to start making improvements mentally and physically because it's something we are more likely to stick to!

How is your relationship with your body? Why are you working out or eating healthy?

Here are a few journaling pages to write down how you feel and set some goals! Remember to be gentle with yourself and know you are not alone in your battles. We can thrive on our fitness journey while also working on our mental health!

THE RIGHT ATTITUDE CAN WEAR ANYTHING

I used to be terrified when I entered the dressing room to try on clothes. I was afraid of looking in the mirror and seeing something I didn't like. I'd go to Target and try on every cute bathing suit and not like any of them because I thought they made me look bad. When I realized it wasn't my body that was the problem, just the way I *looked* at my body, I started to enjoy trying on clothes again.

Having confidence is the BEST, and I mean the best thing in the world! Nothing makes a woman more beautiful than the belief that she is just that.

The next time you go shopping for clothes, use some of my tried-and-true strategies for making the outing what it should be: FUN!

- Listen to music that makes you feel like Beyoncé.

- Remember that our bodies are vehicles to keep us alive. Your body does not completely define you.

- Say out loud 5 times "I AM HOT!" and "THERE IS NO ONE LIKE ME!"

What physical features do you LOVE about yourself? Fill in the outline on the next page by drawing or writing about what gives you the most confidence when you flaunt it!

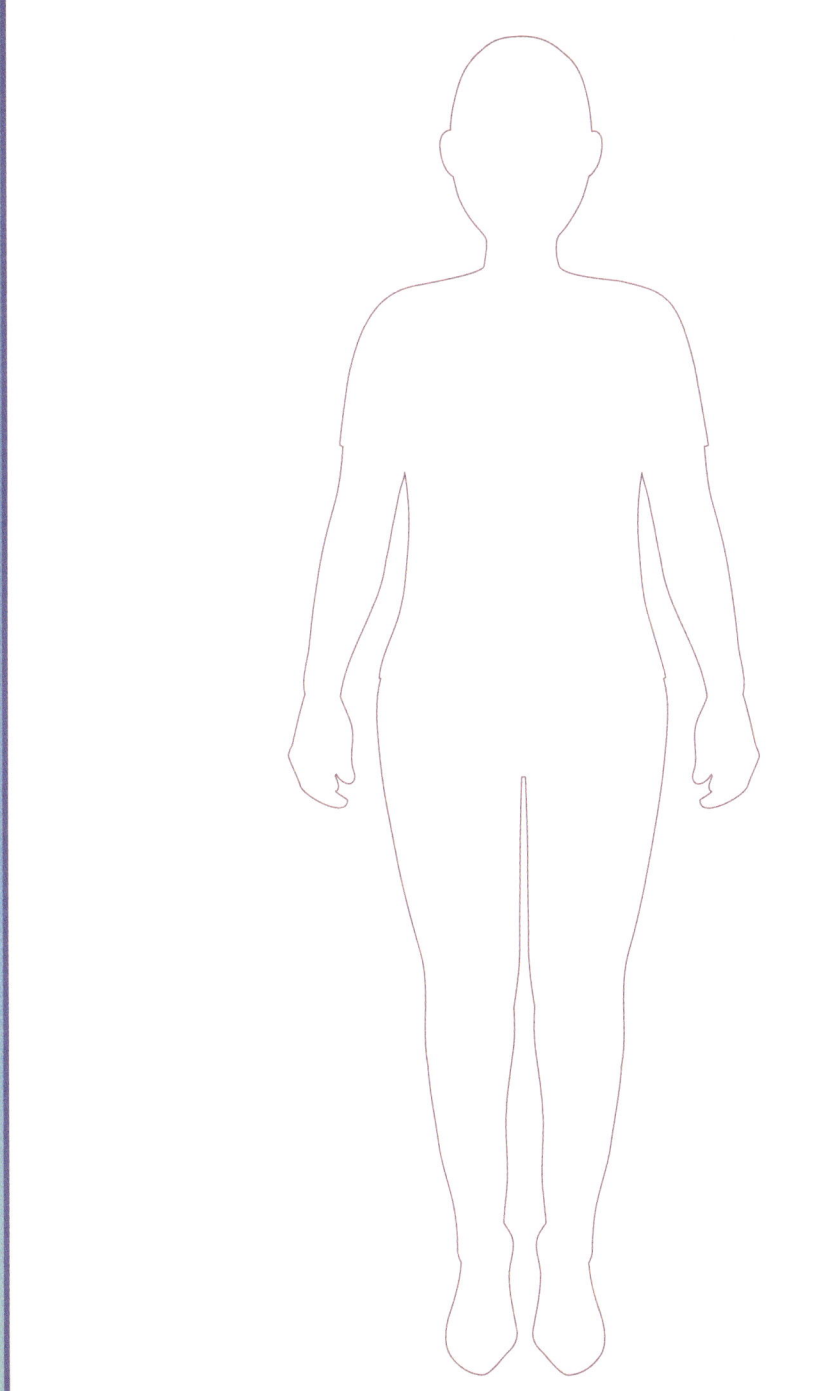

MAKING FITNESS FUN

Working out doesn't have to be stressful or frustrating in order to be a good workout! In fact, working out should be something fun to do, not something forced! Whether it leaves you feeling superstrong or simply clears your head, move your body in a way that feels right to you! I love lifting heavy things (weight training), going on walks, and yoga! I tried Pilates once and bruised my leg from the machine. It was all sorts of confusing for me, so I never went back. At the end of the day, learn to appreciate and be grateful for what YOUR body can do. Never compare your fitness journey to anyone else's; just be the best you there is!

I used to look at exercise as a way to change my body. I now work out to feel empowered and take care of the temple that is my body. I know how to rest, listen to my body, and fuel myself. You're still worthy regardless of what workouts you do or foods you put into your body. Nobody should make you feel bad about what you are or aren't doing. You should do it for you because it makes you feel good!

Set a fitness goal for yourself this month. It's okay to start small! It can be as simple as "I want to run one mile without stopping." Think about what you can do, little by little, each week to reach that goal. It always helps to break things into smaller pieces!

MY GOAL:

....

....

WEEK 1:

....

WEEK 2:

....

WEEK 3:

....

WEEK 4:

....

MY PROGRESS THIS MONTH:

....

....

....

....

To help get you motivated, check out some of my favorite songs to blast while I'm working out. See if they help get your heart rate going, too, or even make a playlist of your own!

My Fitness Playlist

"Powerful" – *Major Lazer (feat. Ellie Goulding & Tarrus Riley)*
"Diva" – *Beyoncé*
"Runaway (U & I)" – *Galantis*
"This Is What You Came For" – *Calvin Harris (feat. Rihanna)*
"Slide" – *Calvin Harris (feat. Frank Ocean & Migos)*

MAD ABOUT MATCHA

I love matcha. I don't really remember when I discovered it, but I did some research on this miracle tea and never looked back. Matcha is powdered green tea leaves that you can use to make drinks or add in baking! It gives you energy without the crash or jitters, calms your mind, boosts metabolism, and is great for your skin!

Here are my favorite ways to use matcha! Try out these recipes and add some notes on what you liked—or include ideas for changing it up next time you make it.

Matcha Latte

Add 1 tsp matcha to your milk of choice. You can use a blender for the matcha or stir it in. It's up to you!

Notes: ....

Matcha Protein Smoothie

½ cup frozen banana

½ cup frozen cauliflower

½ cup frozen spinach

1 tsp matcha

1 cup almond milk

1 scoop of protein powder

Add all ingredients to your blender and set on high speed until smooth.

Notes: ....

Matcha Energy Balls

    4–5 pitted dates

    ½ cup raw walnuts

    1 tsp matcha

    ½ cup shredded coconut

    1 tbsp almond butter

In a food processor, combine all ingredients and form into balls.

Notes: ....

BEST BODY BINGO

Remember to be good to your body. Rip out the next page and tape it somewhere you'll see it every day. When you do something positive for your body—that includes your body *image*!—cross out the action on the board on the next page. When you get bingo (four items crossed out in a row: vertical, horizontal, or diagonal), treat yourself to something fun! You can even photocopy it and challenge a friend to see who gets Best Body Bingo first.

Smile at your reflection	Wear an outfit that makes you feel beautiful	Try a new fitness routine	Prepare a balanced meal for yourself
Try a new food	Accept a compliment without putting yourself down	Go out without any makeup on	Wear an outfit that shows your "flaws" and rock it anyway
Take a walk outside	Try some deep-breathing exercises	Eat some veggies every day for a week	Get into the habit of applying sunscreen every morning
Get eight hours of sleep every night for a week	Blast your favorite song and dance like no one's watching	Indulge in a relaxing bubble bath	Spend at least twenty minutes stretching

STAY HYDRATED, FAM!

Keeping hydrated is key for health and well-being. Our bodies are 60 percent water and our blood is 90 percent water. Water delivers oxygen throughout the body and helps support the kidney and liver functions. It flushes body waste, regulates body temperature, and our digestive system depends upon it. Let's set a goal to drink 1 liter of water a day! Color in the water bottle below to track your progress for the first day.

Here are my favorite benefits of drinking water:

1. Boosts skin health (makes skin glow, and helps with inflammation)

2. Makes minerals and nutrients accessible

3. Boosts performance during exercise

4. Helps to prevent and treat headaches

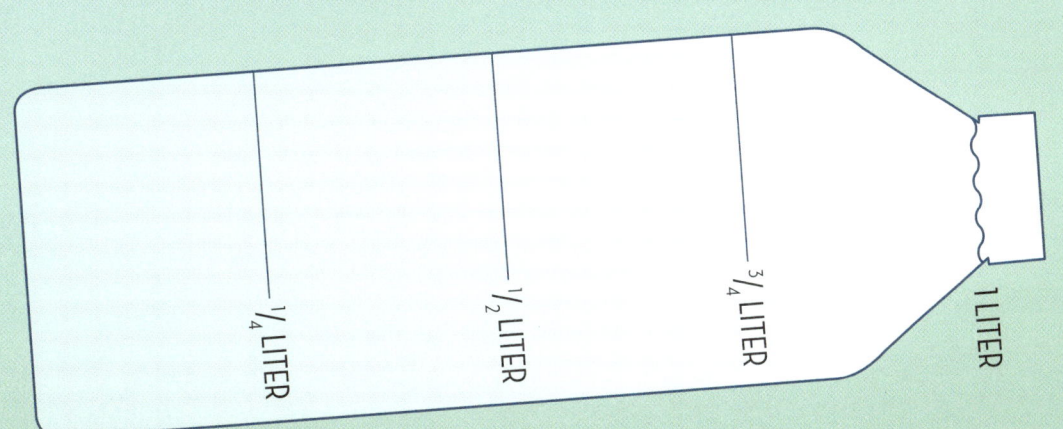

SPIRIT

FLAWS AND ALL

You cannot give up yourself to make someone else happy. I think we can get this idea in our heads that we need to be perfect all the time, when in reality, us being imperfect is what makes us truly beautiful. Don't aspire to be a perfect person because there is no such thing. Be real. Be YOU. Don't hide any part of yourself. Learning to accept and embrace the things you perceive as "flaws" is self-love.

Write down some of your traits that you've always thought of as flaws. Then, in the box next to each one, write how you can embrace this "flaw" and transform it into something amazing and special about you.

I have always been a little insecure of my nose. I don't love how it flares out when I smile, but guess what, I know that God made me this way for a reason . . . nobody else looks like me. (HOW COOL!) I have learned to embrace this and do not want to change it because it's what makes me, ME!

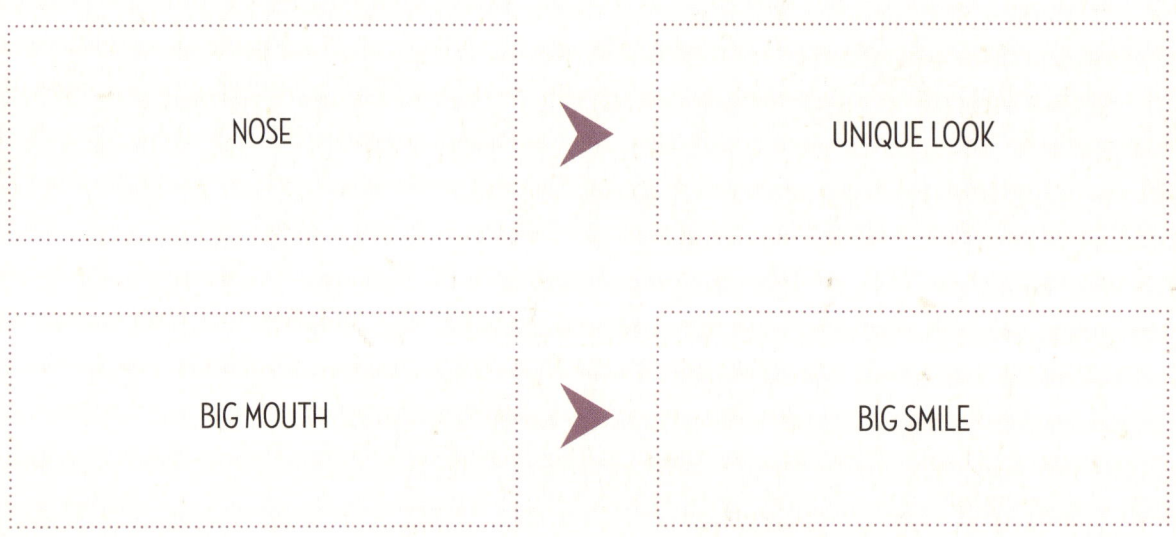

SHOWING GRATITUDE

Her aura shined
a million colors at once.
Aligned with the heart of God,
she sang in tune with the world
for she knew its way.
She was gratitude.

Before you go to sleep tonight, make a list of 10 things you're grateful for. Get into the habit of making this list, either in writing or just in your head, every night.

1. ....

2. ....

3. ....

4. ....

5. ....

6. ....

7. ....

8. ....

9. ....

10. ....

10 THINGS YOU LOVE ABOUT YOU

She was beautiful.
Not in the way her face looked,
but in the way her heart beat.
Her heart was pure love and light.
It radiated out of her skin
and onto others.

Write down 10 things you love about yourself.

1. ....

2. ....

3. ....

4. ....

5. ....

6. ....

7. ....

8. ....

9. ....

10. ....

CHILDHOOD MEMORIES

*She was her childhood favorite ice cream
rainbow sherbet on a hot summer day,
the feeling of innocence her inner child could hold onto
igniting a fire in her soul*

Remember how you felt being a child? How carefree and innocent you were? The happiness you felt from everything and everyone? How you didn't take anything too personally or let people's actions and words affect the way you viewed yourself? You hardly ever thought about the future or even the past.

You just were.

Honor the child within you, for you were once that person and still are. Do things that make you feel as you once did. That child you remember is enough; you are enough to love.

Write down 5 things that make you feel like a child (like running naked through the sprinkler)!

1. ....

2. ....

3. ....

4. ....

5. ....

How can you work these things back into your life to remind yourself to let loose and be more carefree?

QUIZ: WHICH SEASON MATCHES YOUR SPIRIT?

Answer these questions to find out your seasonal soul mate!

She was young at heart, but old by soul.
As frosty winter turns to spring
As the snowy ice melts into water
She reminds us that there's always time to change.

Your style can best be described as:

    A. Trendy and colorful

    B. Simple and comfortable

    C. Matching whatever mood you're in that day

    D. Sleek and sophisticated

Among your friends, you're the one most likely to:

    A. Know every guest at a party

    B. Lend an ear

    C. Randomly go MIA and then return like nothing happened

    D. Organize details for a group outing

You prefer to spend most of your free time:

    A. Going to concerts and sporting events

    B. Reading or watching movies

    C. Diving into a new hobby, whether it's yoga or the ukulele

    D. What free time?!

In the future, you can picture yourself as a:

    A. Teacher

    B. Writer

    C. Wildlife photographer

    D. CEO

What's your favorite scent?

    A. Marshmallow

    B. Cinnamon

    C. Lavender

    D. Pumpkin

RESULTS

MOSTLY As - SUMMER
You're cheerful, friendly, and often the life of the party!

MOSTLY Bs - WINTER
You're typically quiet and introverted, though no one is more caring and empathetic.

MOSTLY Cs - SPRING
You can be very unpredictable! You're adventurous and always ready to try something new.

MOSTLY Ds - FALL
You're a natural-born leader: responsible, hardworking—and always busy!

I GOT MOSTLY Ds! I am Fall, which is so fitting since I was born in autumn and am a fall baby!

NATURE JOURNAL

Her soul lit up a dark room
making each morning beautiful and bright
a soul that spoke without words
making each moment fleeting
a content feeling of serenity
Her soul lit up the night sky
for she was the moon and stars we gaze upon.

I love using the beauty of nature to take some time and reflect. My favorite way to do this is to take a walk or even simply sit outside and write down what I see or feel. Use these pages to try out nature journaling for yourself! I've added some ideas along the way to help get your creative juices flowing!

Natural Fun

What do you love to do that does NOT involve any screens, gadgets, or technology?

Sense Focusing

Focus on each of your 5 senses, one at a time. Really let yourself hone in on each one and feel what your body is telling you in this moment. No detail is too small.

WHAT DO YOU *SEE*?
....
....

WHAT DO YOU *HEAR*?
....
....

WHAT CAN YOU *SMELL*?
....
....

WHAT CAN YOU *TOUCH*?
....
....

WHAT CAN YOU *TASTE*? (DON'T GET TOO CRAZY WITH THIS ONE—HOPEFULLY, YOU HAVE A SNACK OR WATER BOTTLE TO HELP YOU OUT HERE!)
....
....

Use what you've written about your 5 senses to write a poem.

The Art of Nature

Find something beautiful outside and sketch it here. Don't worry if you're not an experienced artist. This is just for you and there's no one here to judge it!

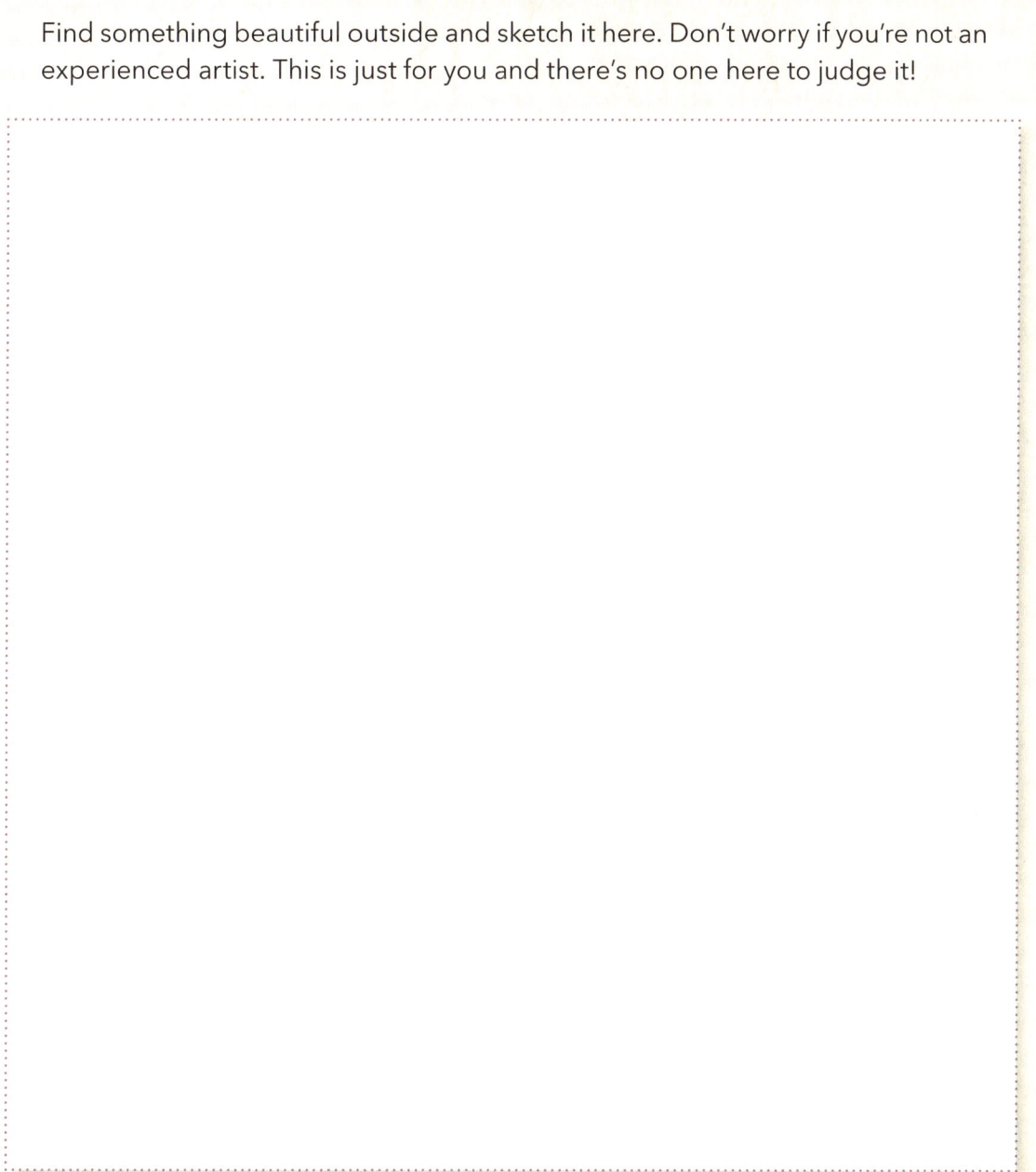

Nature Experiences

Use the remaining pages to complete your Nature Journal with anything else you want to reflect upon while in the beauty of the outdoors.

....

....

....

....

....

....

....

....

....

....

....

....

....

....

....

....

....

she felt emotion like
a rainstorm after a drought.
soaked up every last drop
to make something grow
but when there were no seeds planted
she waited on a rose
that would only turn to thorns.

QUIZ: HOW CAN YOU GIVE BACK?

Giving back is something I like to implement in my everyday life. Whether it's big or small, doing things for others is going to take the focus off you and put your energy into something great. The first step is to find out what it is that you're passionate about!

Take this quiz to get some great ideas for how you can start giving back to others.

Choose the role you think fits you best:
- A. Nurturer
- B. Organizer
- C. Leader

Which challenge would you happily take on?
- A. Wrangling a large, energetic Labrador retriever into a bath
- B. Reorganizing hundreds of items to create a new filing system
- C. Finding a great location to host an event for free

What is most important for helping others in need?
- A. Spreading cheer, comfort, and positivity
- B. Providing education
- C. Offering financial support

You're happiest when you're surrounded by:
- A. Animals
- B. Books
- C. People

RESULTS

MOSTLY As - ANIMAL ADVOCATE
You love being around furry friends, and you know the joy they can bring to others! Consider helping out at a local animal shelter, fostering a pet, or becoming a volunteer dog walker or pet-sitter for someone who is unable to do it themselves.

MOSTLY Bs - LIBRARY LOVER
Public libraries can often use help from dedicated volunteers—and you don't even have to be book-crazy to get involved (though if you are, even better!). You may help out with shelving items, filing and organizing, creating displays, or even assisting with public programs.

MOSTLY Cs - FUNDRAISER FUN
You have a can-do, go-getter attitude, perfect for coordinating a big fundraising event. Choose a charity close to your heart and think of a way to raise money, whether it's a bake sale, garage sale, car wash, or even a concert for local musicians!

Now that you have some ideas, you're ready to get out there and start giving back!

I LOVE animals and baking, so I have volunteered at a dog shelter and made homemade dog treats! I'm also planning on becoming a Sunday school teacher at my local church. You don't have to donate money to help a cause! You can just be a part of a movement by using your voice and actions for good!

GOOD DEED OF THE DAY JAR

There are also great ways to give back that don't require a big time commitment. Even the smallest of acts can make a HUGE difference in someone's life. No good deed goes unnoticed.

Cut along the dotted lines to create slips of paper with a random act of kindness on each one. Fill a jar with the paper slips and pick one out at random anytime you want to spread a little goodness in the world. The one you choose is your Good Deed of the Day!

Pay for the order of the person behind you in line.	Write a social media post about a local business or organization you love.
Leave sticky notes with uplifting messages on all the mirrors in a public restroom.	Leave a note in a library book you love, recommending it to the next reader.
Complete a chore for someone without telling them.	Give someone a genuine compliment.
Leave a treat with a note in the mailbox for your mail carrier.	Buy your best friend his or her favorite candy, just because.
Strike up a conversation with someone new at school.	Visit a local park and pick up any litter.
Tape a dollar to a vending machine with a note that says, "This one's on me!"	Grab some chalk and write a positive message on a public sidewalk.
Send a postcard to a faraway family member.	Cut coupons and leave them taped to shelved items at the grocery store.

FINDING YOUR HOME TEAM

Community is so important. Having a "home team" and people you can count on will make your life so much better. One of my mentors and a person who I look up to in life told me this: "A home team is essential. It is like a personal army to help us combat what life throws at us. Only 'enlist' those who are both loyal and loving. Have at least one fearless fighter and a few faithful soldiers who know how to have fun and not get too serious about things, and you're set!"

Do you have a home team of your own? Write their names and one thing you love about each of them here. You can even go one step further and turn what you write here into a personal note or text to each of them, expressing gratitude for your friendship.

If your team isn't quite complete yet, write down the qualities you most value in a friend. Think about who you know who may have some of these qualities—it might be worth getting to know them better!

FRIEND'S NAME	DESCRIPTION

OUR SOCIAL MEDIA SELVES

It's important to hang out with people who know how to really LIVE and not get sucked into the social media trap of trying to look cool all the time. I know how hard it is to find a few people you can really trust and connect with. It's something that gets harder and harder with social media making it almost impossible to differentiate what's real and what's fake! In fact, let's do a little experiment.

Take a minute to look at your own social media accounts. Pretend you're a total stranger looking at your posts, photos, and comments for the first time. Write down a few words, phrases, or sentences you would use to describe the person you see online.

Now, think about the real life behind your posts. What words or phrases would you use to describe your true self? How would close friends or family describe you? What part of yourself do people know nothing about if they're just basing their perceptions of you from social media? What are they missing—good OR bad?

....
....
....
....
....
....
....
....
....
....
....
....

It just goes to show how social media is *never* the whole story. We all want to put our best selves forward when sharing things online—but there is so much more to all of us than what meets the eye.

TOXIC FRIENDSHIPS

I have put my trust in the wrong people at times and had to learn a few lessons as a result. It can be hurtful, but sometimes we can't take it personally. Everyone is going through a battle of their own, so the best thing to do is be kind and show love to everyone, even your "enemies." It will only make you stronger and help you grow as an individual.

In high school and my early adult life, I experienced many friend groups that were not built on solid foundations. They were almost "formed" or strategic to give off a certain look. I just thought these people really liked me and wanted to be my friends. I realized I had to separate myself from these toxic friendships for my own well-being.

Think about the friendships that have come in and out of your life. Have any of them ever made you feel you weren't good enough? Did anyone ever act like a friend to your face, but tell a different story with their actions?

Imagine you're writing a letter to one of those people. Now is your chance to say what you've always wanted to say, to let them know how they made you feel. Let those negative emotions flow out of you and onto the page. Don't hold back!

THANK YOU FOR BEING A FRIEND

Soon after I walked away from those toxic "friend" groups, I met some amazing people that truly wanted to see me shine. They did not want to put out my light or extinguish me. These are the types of friends to surround yourself with. Remember that glowing women can help other women glow and still be lit themselves. Friends should encourage each other, lift each other up, and want to see you SHINE!

Think back to your home team. Who stands out as the person who has *always* been there for you and has accepted you just as you are? Who has seen you through your failures and your successes? Who lifts you up and makes you feel like you can do anything?

Write this person a letter to let that person know how much they mean to you and how their love and support has helped you stay true to yourself even when others tried to tear you down. This letter may be one that you actually want to share!

MY FINAL MUSINGS

Wow! You have done SO much work. You've reorganized, volunteered, spread positivity, accomplished fitness goals, tried new recipes, confronted your insecurities, spent some time connecting with nature, reflected on your friendships, and so much more—all while remaining true to yourself and what's important to you. Pshh, no big deal!

You should be ridiculously proud of everything you have accomplished. And guess what? We're all *always* working on ourselves. After we climb one mountain, there's probably another one waiting for us at the top. We're constantly growing and learning, so don't be worried if you feel like you still have things to work on. I'd be shocked if you didn't, because I know I do!

Take a moment to give yourself some serious kudos for all you've done to nurture your mind, body, and spirit. These last pages are for you to fill with any final thoughts you want to get down on paper. Think back over this entire journey: What was hardest for you? What did you maybe expect to struggle with, only to find that you totally crushed it? What have these activities shown you about yourself? I hope they've reminded you what I know to be true: You are strong, beautiful, powerful, and worthy of being the absolute best YOU that you can be.

ACKNOWLEDGMENTS

This book would not be possible without my family, friends, and team cheering me on.

My family, the Fosters, have been the greatest support team I've had my entire life. I want to thank my mom and dad, Laurie and Steve, for helping me with the most mundane tasks that nobody else would and for just being people I could always talk to. My sister and brother, Lizzie and Michael, for always loving me even when I was probably a pain in the butt. My family has cared for me through the hardest times in my life, and I wouldn't be here without them.

My friends, who have inspired me, reminded me who I was, and never stopped being there for me . . . you know who you are! Big thanks especially to Anastasia Jessica, Brianne Erman, Madison Clark, Sierra Furtado, and Teala Dunn for our wonderful photos together in this book!

My team! Colette, Eddie, Nikki, Jade, and Sophie, you guys are the best and I couldn't be more grateful to work with you to make amazing things happen.

I want to thank all of you reading this who have stuck by me and supported me throughout the years. It means more to me than you'll ever know.

And lastly, thank you to Little Bee Books, for publishing this book and helping make my vision come to life!

Meredith Foster, a California native, is a YouTube star, influencer, and entrepreneur. With a combined digital audience of over ten million followers, she has worked with top media and production companies, and has partnered with some of the biggest lifestyle and beauty brands in the world.

Meredith spreads self-love and encourages her audience to celebrate who they are. She enjoys cooking and baking delicious healthy treats, meditating, traveling, and fitness.

"THE HELLFIRE CLUB"

Written by
JAI NITZ

Pencils & inks by
COLTON WORLEY

Colors by
ROMULO FAJARDO JR.
CARLOS LOPEZ

Letters by
SIMON BOWLAND

Collection cover by
COLTON WORLEY

Special thanks to
DAVID GRACE
at Green Hornet Inc.

Collection design by
JASON ULLMEYER

ISBN-10: 1-60690-224-5   ISBN-13: 978-1-60690-224-0   First Printing   10 9 8 7 6 5 4 3 2 1

KATO™ ORIGINS VOLUME TWO: THE HELLFIRE CLUB. First printing. Contains materials originally published in Kato Origins #6-11. Published by Dynamite Entertainment. 155 Ninth Ave. Suite B, Runnemede, NJ 08078. Copyright © 2011 The Green Hornet, Inc. All rights reserved. Kato, The Green Hornet, Black Beauty, and the hornet logos are trademarks of The Green Hornet, Inc. www.thegreenhornet.com. Dynamite, Dynamite Entertainment & The Dynamite Entertainment colophon ® 2011 DFI. All Rights Reserved. All names, characters, events, and locales in this publication are entirely fictional. Any resemblance to actual persons (living or dead), events or places, without satiric intent, is coincidental. No portion of this book may be reproduced by any means (digital or print) without the written permission of Dynamite Entertainment except for review purposes. The scanning, uploading and distribution of this book via the Internet or via any other means without the permission of the publisher is illegal and punishable by law. Please purchase only authorized electronic editions, and do not participate in or encourage electronic piracy of copyrighted materials. **Printed in China.**

For media rights, foreign rights, promotions, licensing, and advertising: marketing@dynamite.net

DYNAMITE ENTERTAINMENT

WWW.DYNAMITE.NET

NICK BARRUCCI • PRESIDENT
JUAN COLLADO • CHIEF OPERATING OFFICER
JOSEPH RYBANDT • EDITOR
JOSH JOHNSON • CREATIVE DIRECTOR
RICH YOUNG • DIRECTOR OF BUSINESS DEVELOPMENT
JASON ULLMEYER • SENIOR DESIGNER
JOSH GREEN • TRAFFIC COORDINATOR
CHRIS CANIANO • PRODUCTION ASSISTANT

Issue six cover by **COLTON WORLEY**

Issue six alternate cover by **FRANCESCO FRANCAVILLA**

DREAMLAND GARDENS JAZZ CLUB, BRONZEVILLE, CHICAGO, 1942.

I LIKE JAZZ. IT WAS THE FIRST AMERICAN TRADITION I EMBRACED.

I SEE A DIFFERENT JAZZ BAND IN BRONZEVILLE TWICE A WEEK.

ONE TIME I SAW ETHEL WATERS AT THE BLUE NOTE.

LAST MONTH I SAW JAY McSHANN BRING THE "KANSAS CITY SOUND" TO CHICAGO. HE HAD A HORN PLAYER NAMED CHARLIE PARKER WHO LEFT ME SPEECHLESS.

MUSIC RELAXES ME.

IN JAPAN, MY UNCLE ICHIRO PLAYED THE FOUR-STRING BIWA AND SANG.

THE WHOLE FAMILY WOULD GATHER ROUND TO LISTEN TO MY UNCLE PLAY. THE MUSIC CREATED A TIME FOR FAMILY TOGETHERNESS.

MY FAMILY WAS ALWAYS SO EXCITED FOR THE MUSIC, BUT I WAS ALWAYS RELAXED.

KNOCK KNOCK

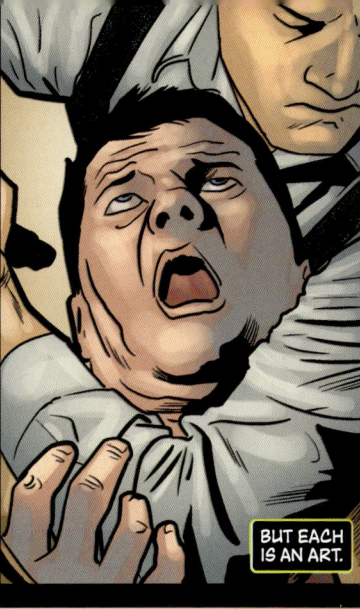

MY LAST NIGHT BEFORE RETURNING HOME, I PASSED AN OPIUM HOUSE.

THERE I SAW MY UNCLE ICHIRO.

HE HAD SOLD HIS BIWA TO PAY FOR HIS ADDICTION.

TEEN DIES AFTER SAVAGE BEATING

Issue seven cover by **COLTON WORLEY**

Issue seven alternate cover by FRANCESCO FRANCAVILLA

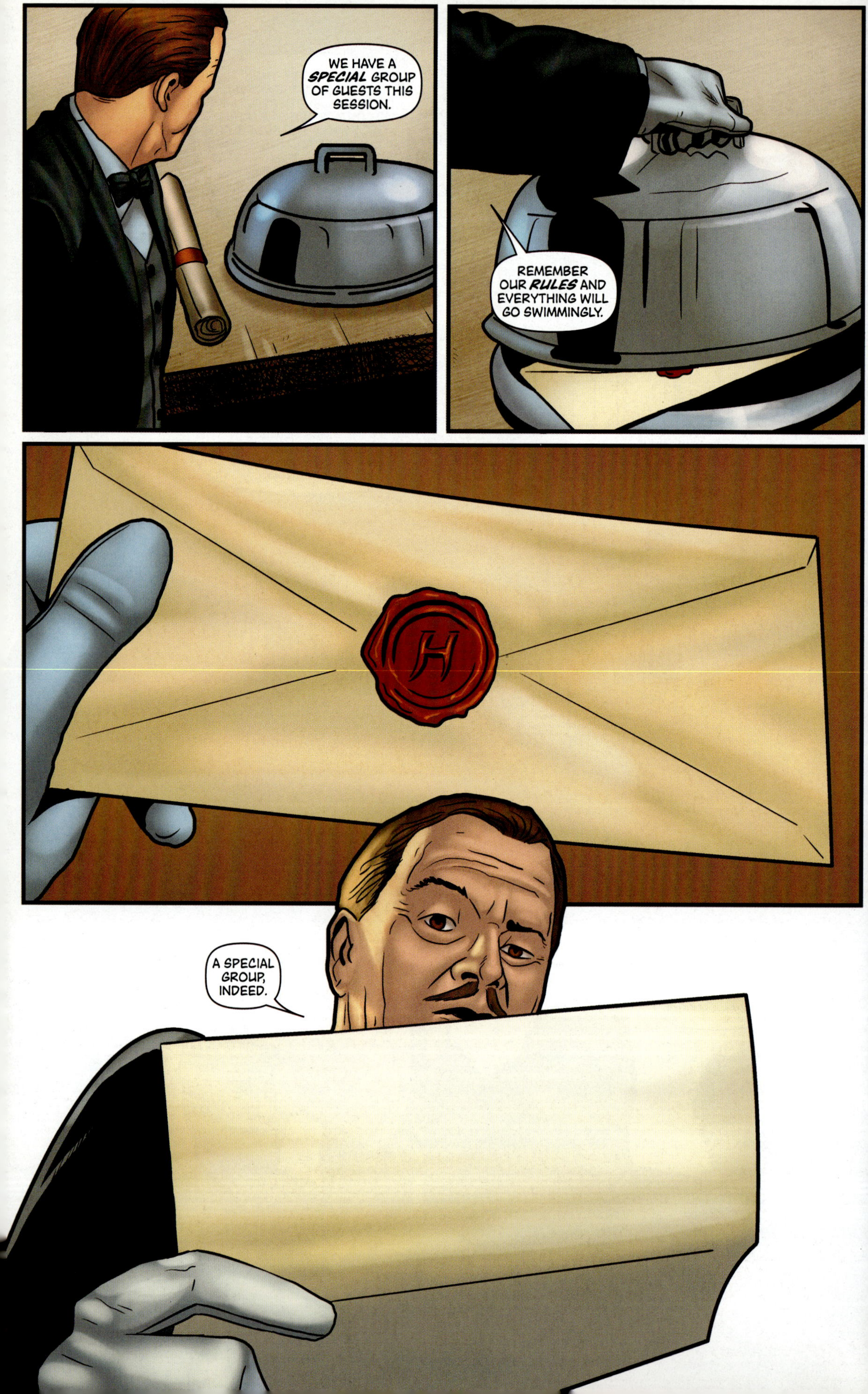

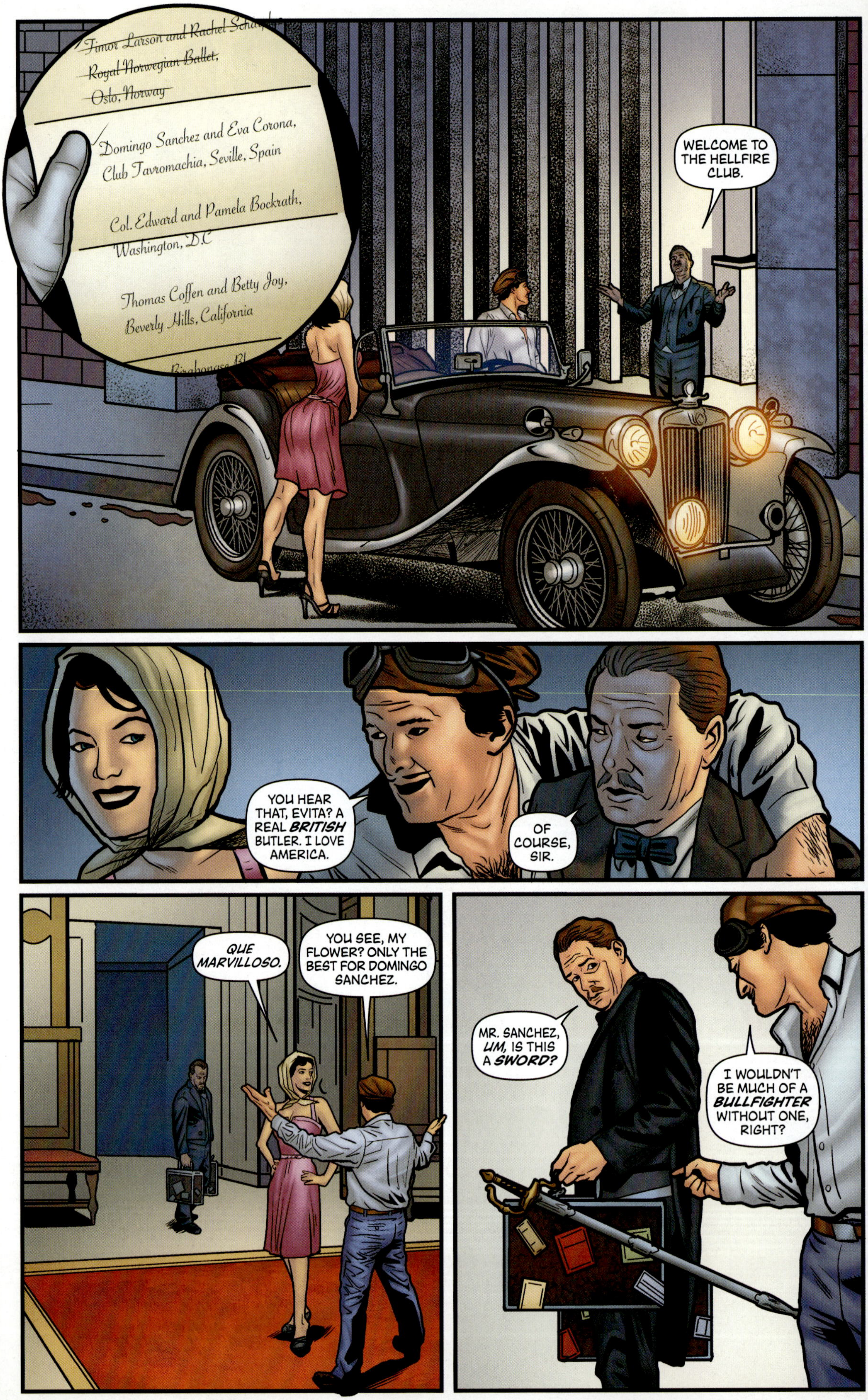

"HRMPH."

"SMALL."

"MR. COFFEN, IT IS AN HONOR TO HAVE YOU AT THE..."

"SAVE IT, REDCAP. THIS TRIP IS FOR *BETTY*, NOT ME. I DON'T PLAN ON INDULGING HER...*PROCLIVITIES* ON MY PROPERTY."

"BUT I STILL LOVE HER, SO SHE GETS WHAT SHE WANTS, NO MATTER HOW *DEPRAVED*."

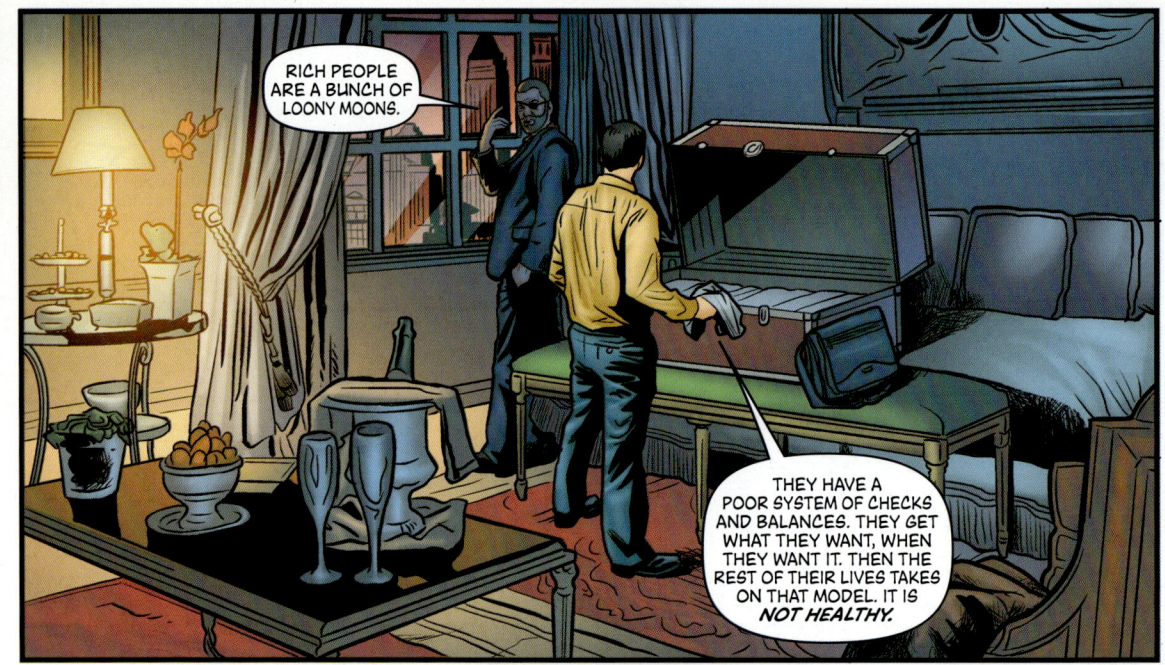

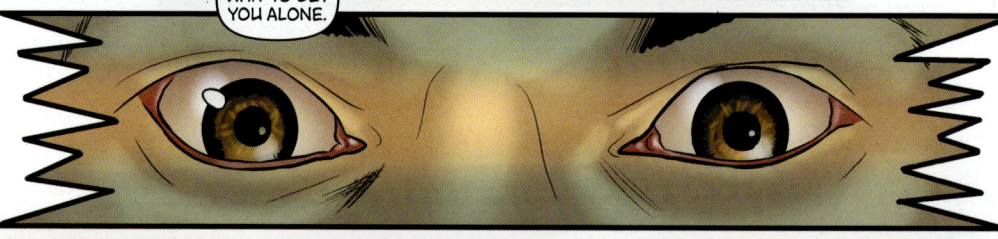

Issue eight cover by COLTON WORLEY

Issue eight alternate cover by FRANCESCO FRANCAVILLA

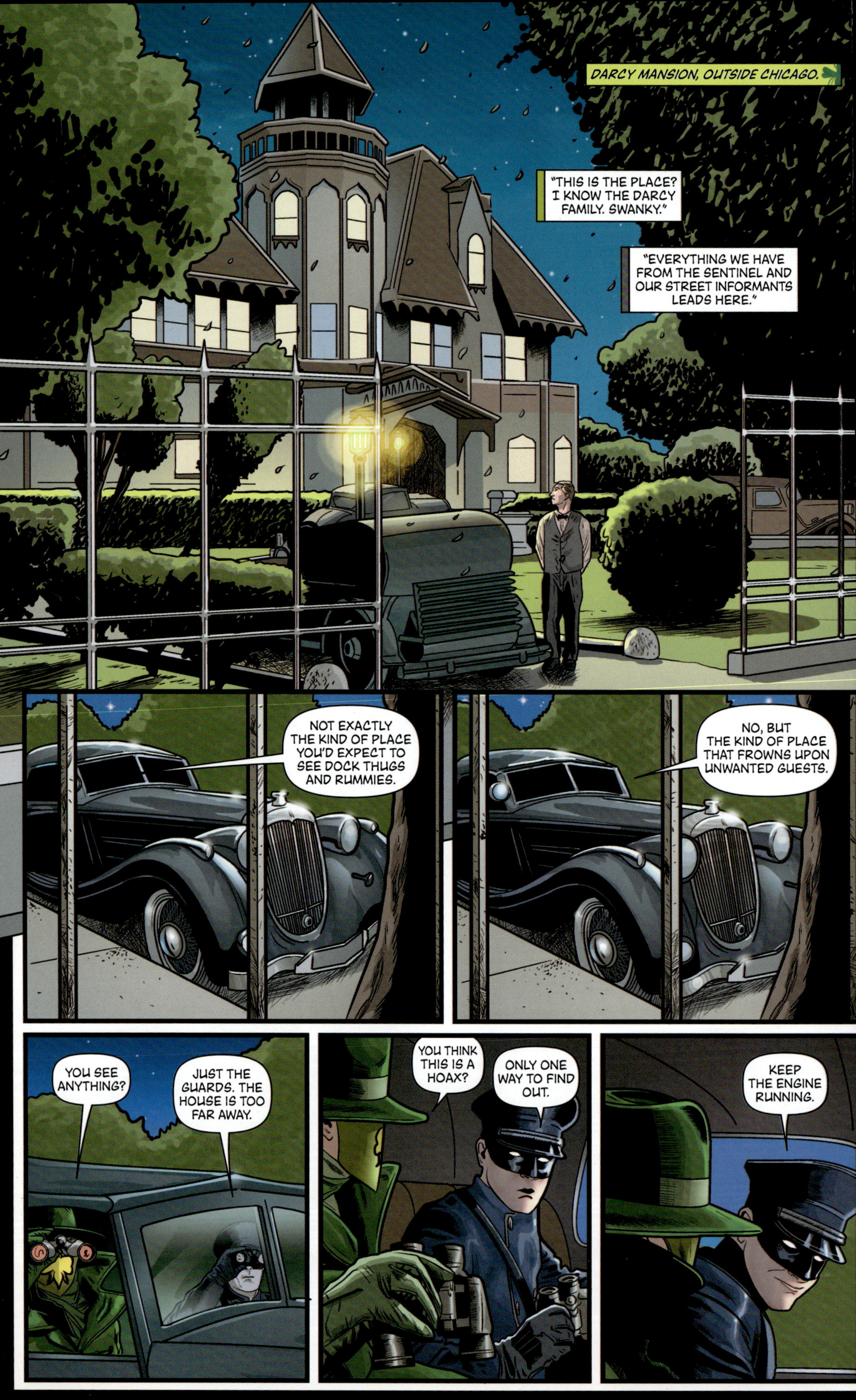

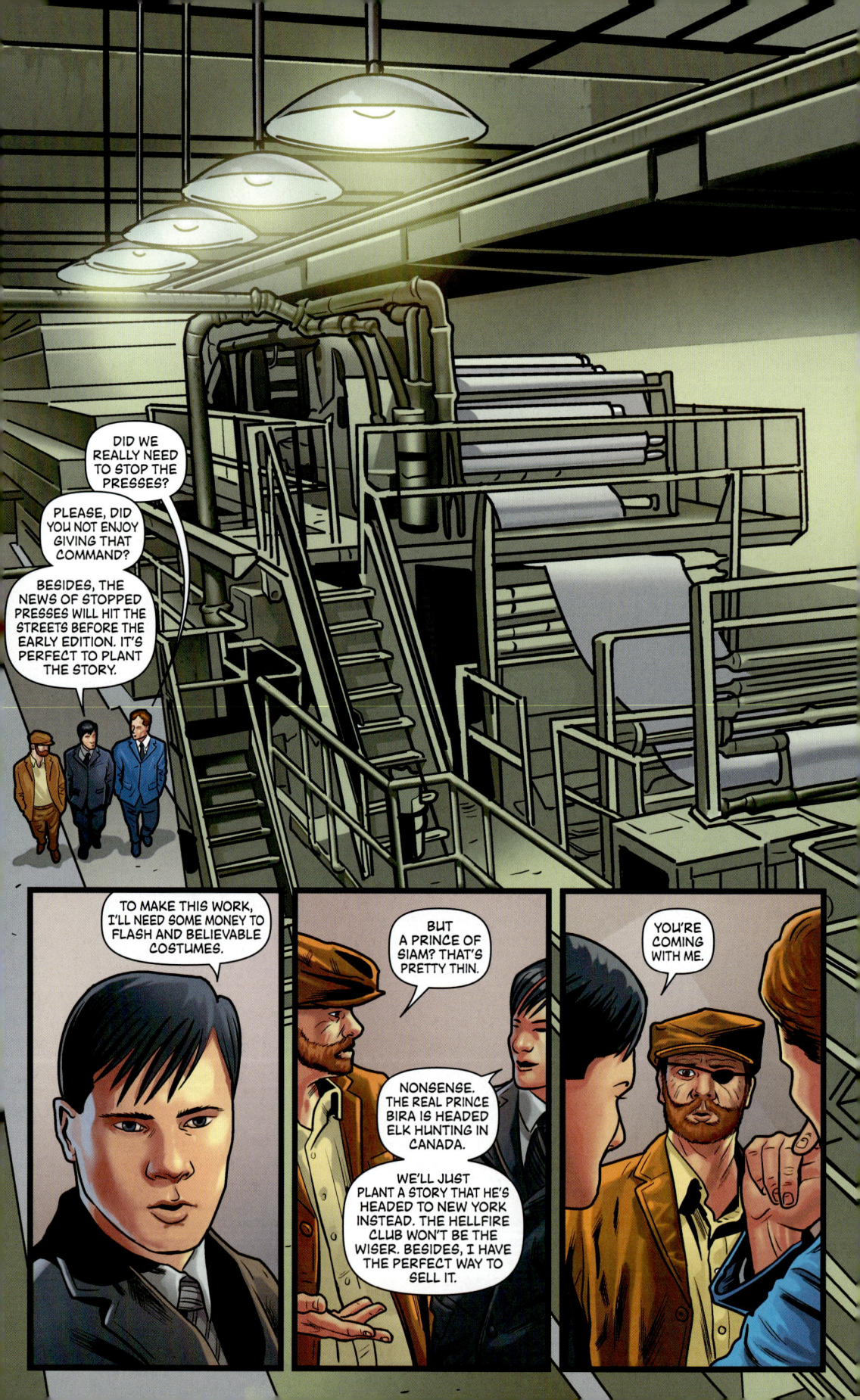

Issue nine cover by **COLTON WORLEY**

Issue nine alternate cover by **FRANCESCO FRANCAVILLA**

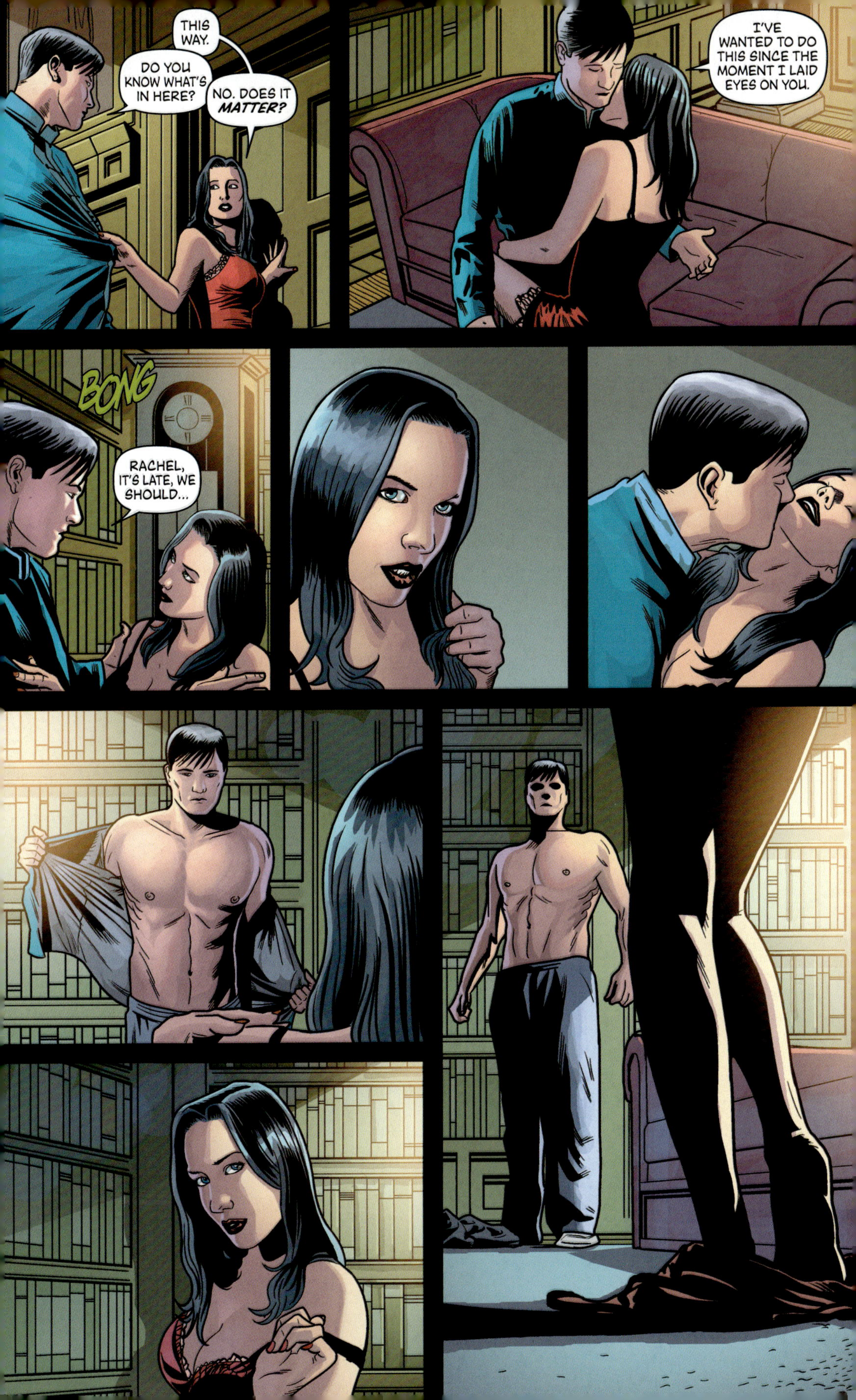

THIS WAY.

DO YOU KNOW WHAT'S IN HERE?

NO. DOES IT *MATTER?*

I'VE WANTED TO DO THIS SINCE THE MOMENT I LAID EYES ON YOU.

BONG

RACHEL, IT'S LATE, WE SHOULD...

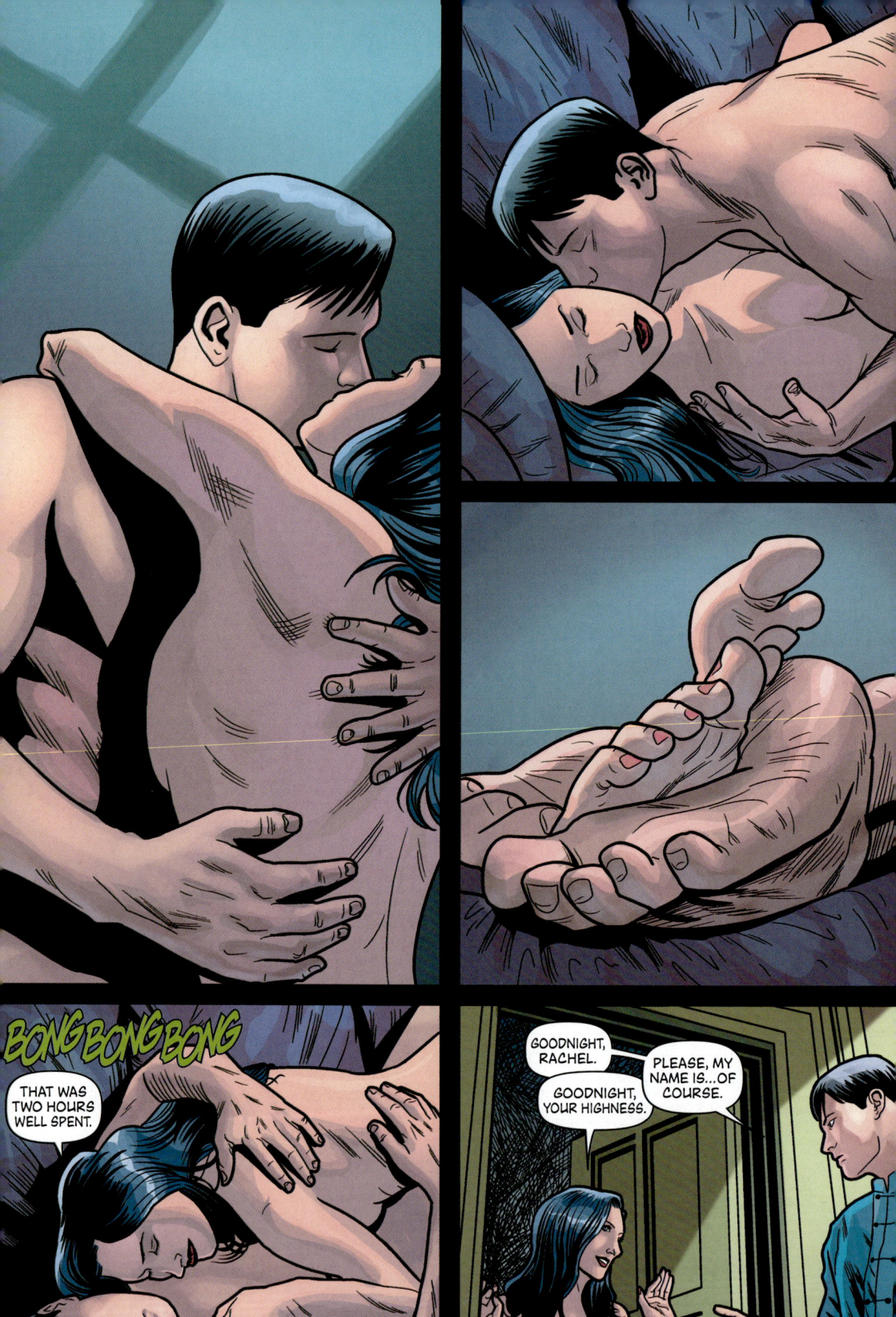

MIDNIGHT SNACK, YOUR HIGHNESS?

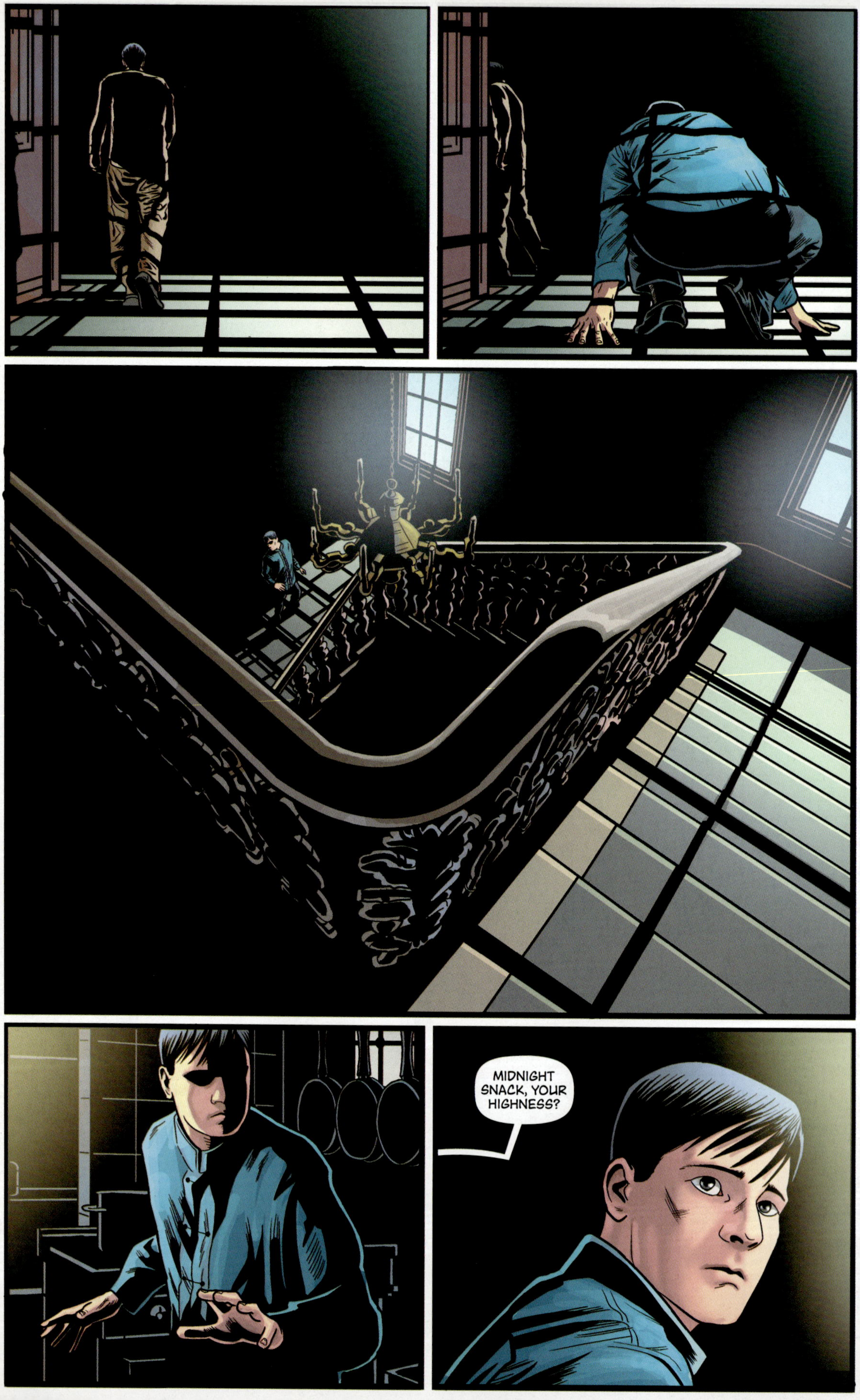

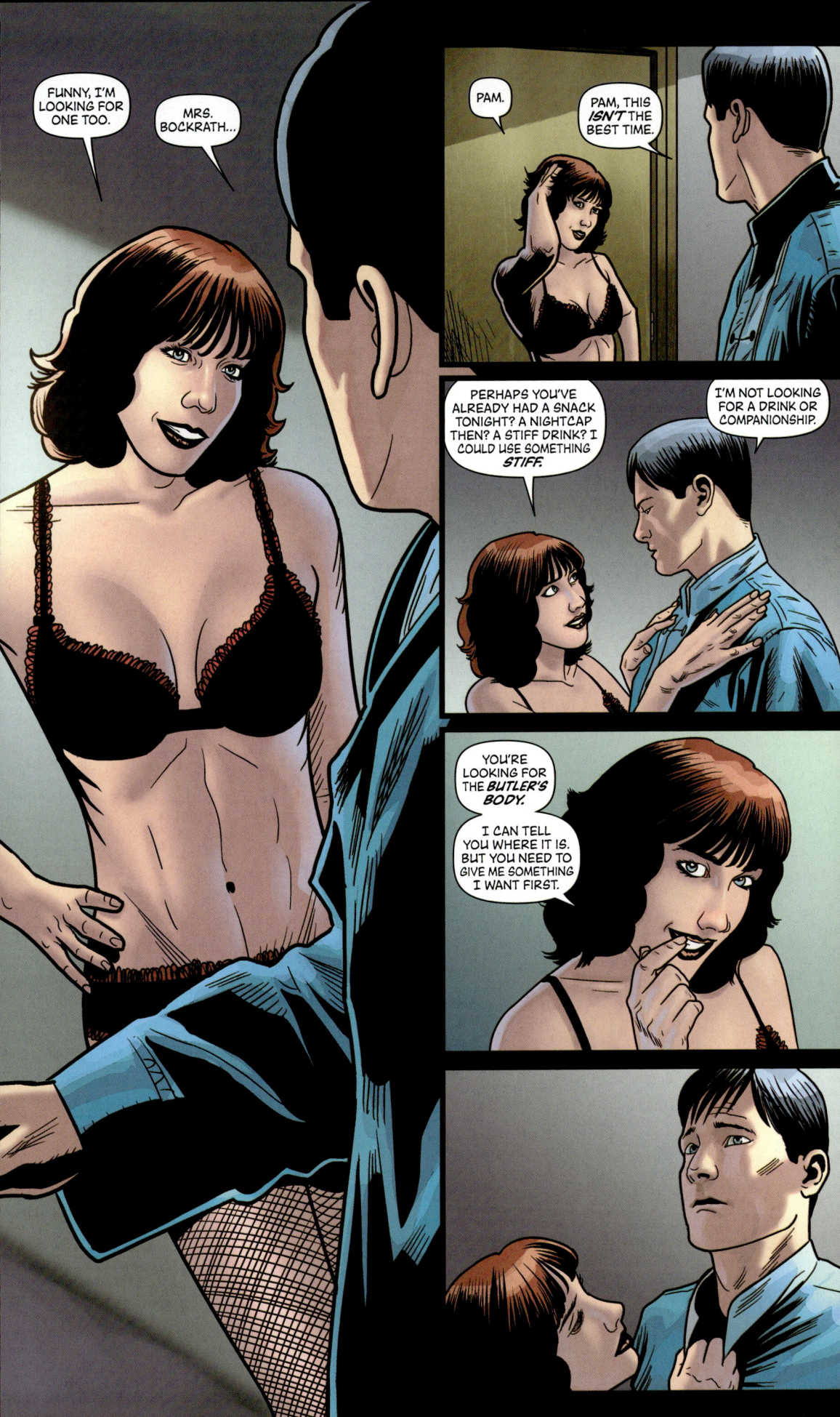

JAMES? JAMES?

GOOD MORNING, ALL. SORRY TO ARRIVE SO LATE TO BREAKFAST.

IT WAS A *LONG* NIGHT, YOUR HIGHNESS.

FOR *SOME* OF US.

Issue ten cover by **COLTON WORLEY**

Issue tent alternate cover by FRANCESCO FRANCAVILLA

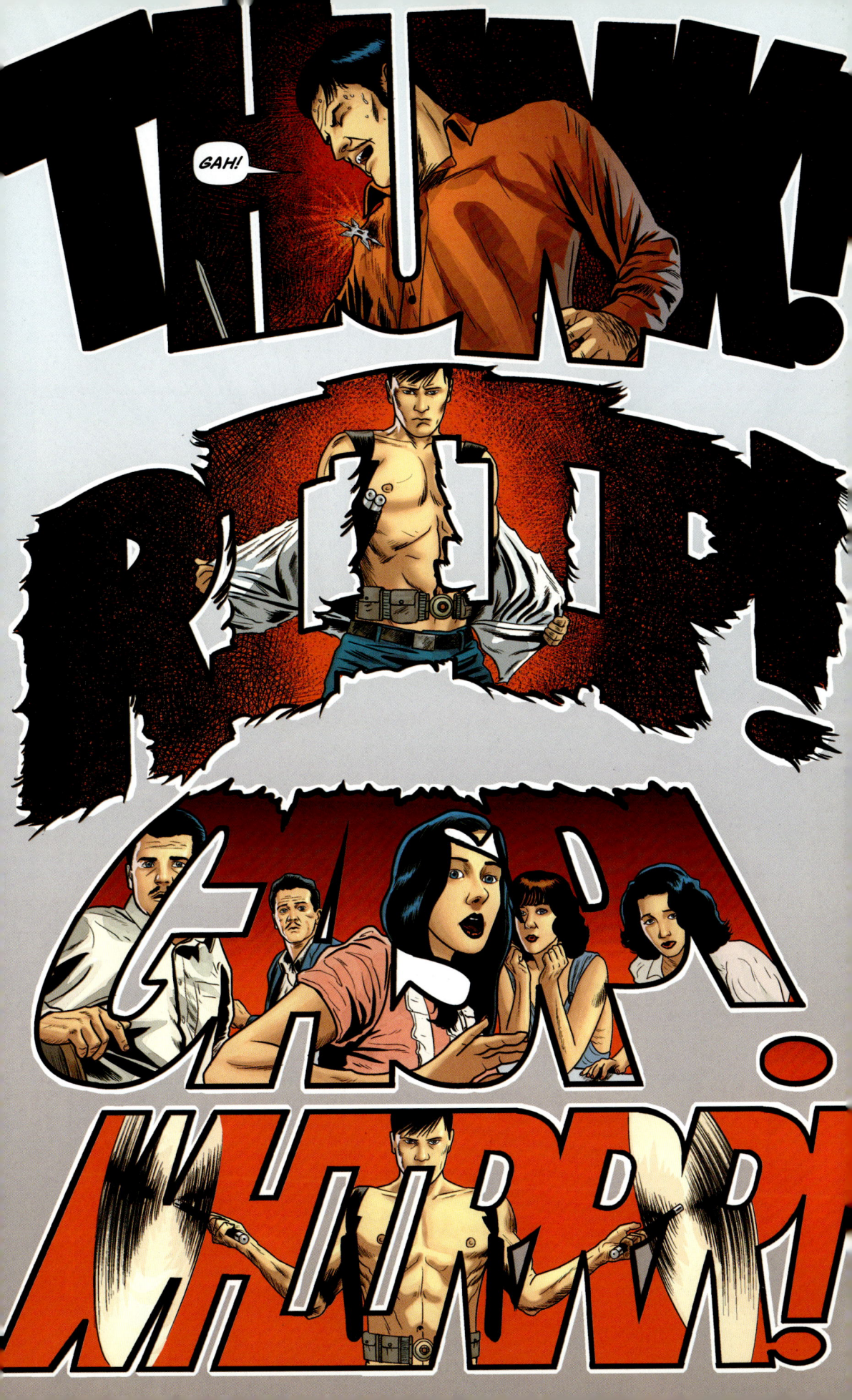

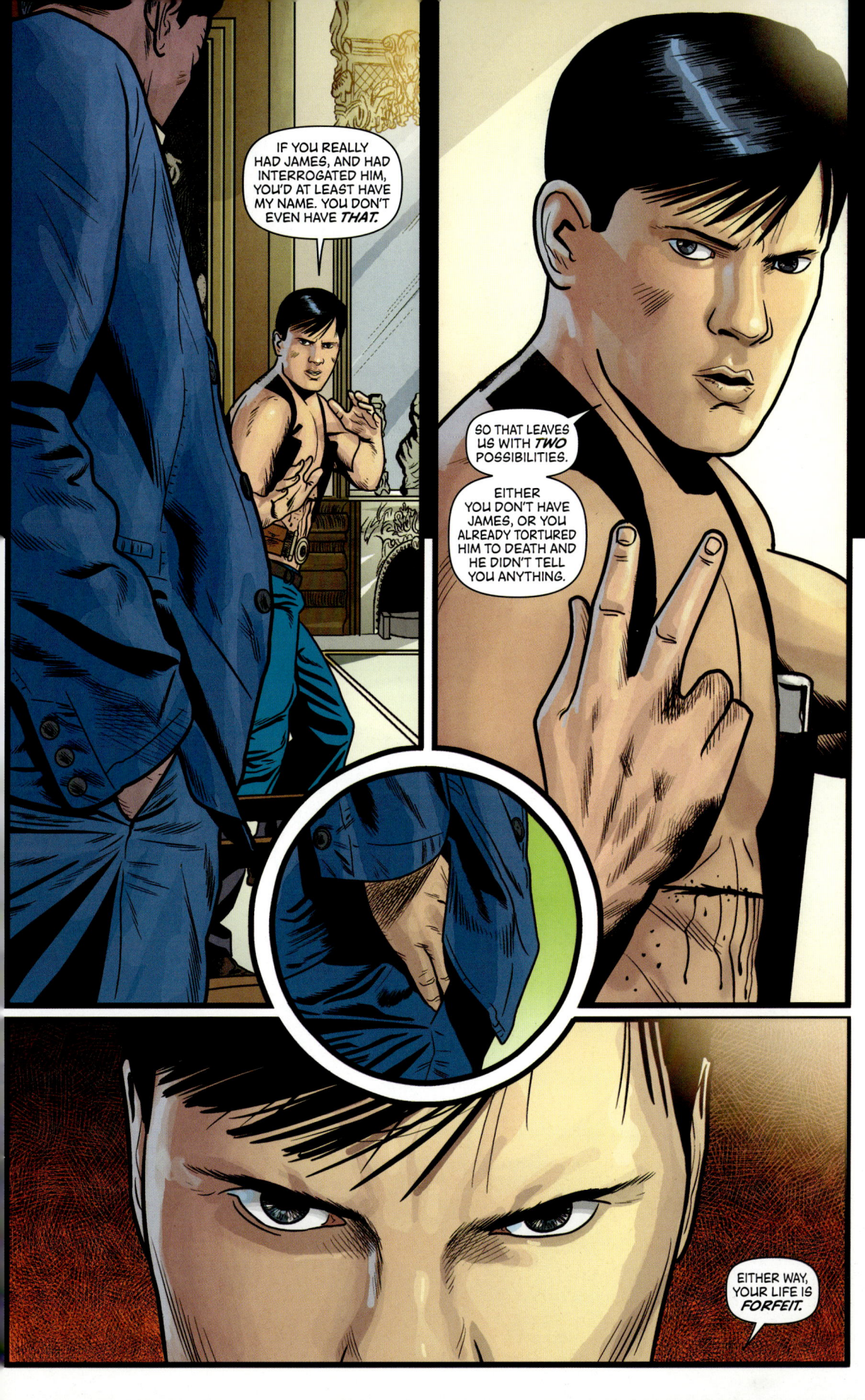

Issue eleven cover by **COLTON WORLEY**

Issue eleven alternate cover by **FRANCESCO FRANCAVILLA**

FIND HIM.

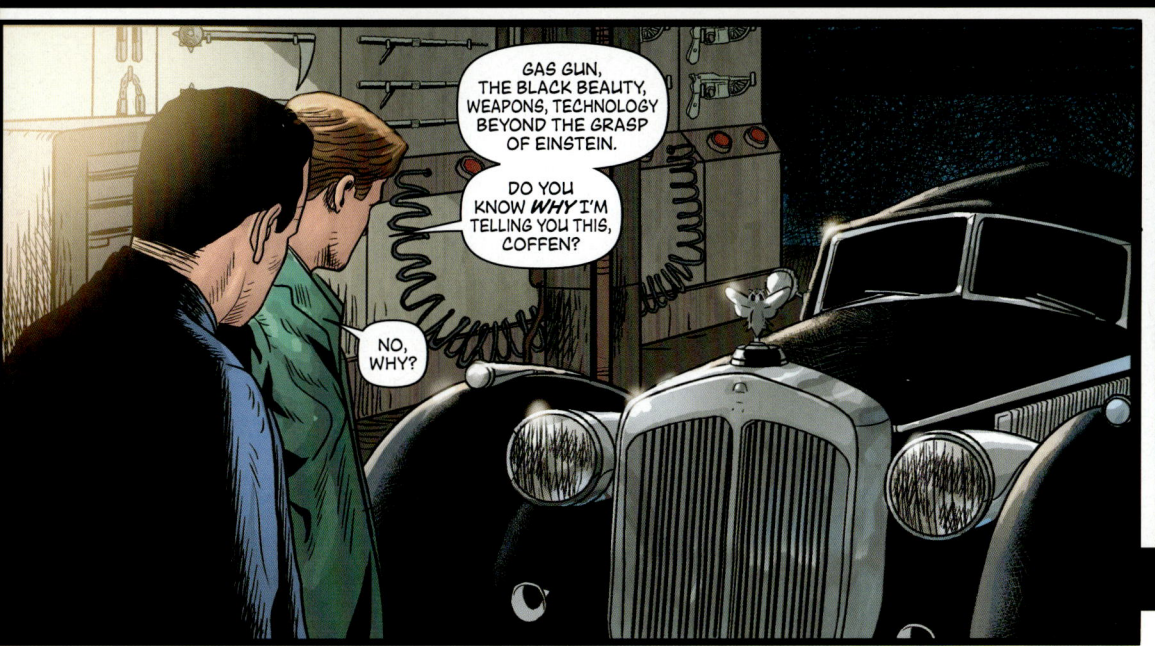

KEVIN SMITH presents THE GREEN HORNET!

  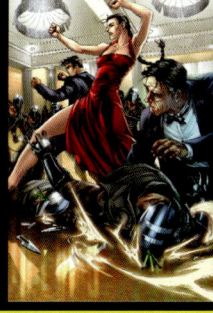 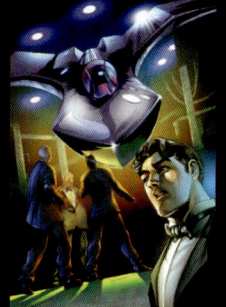 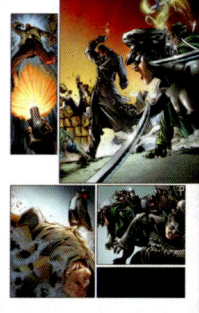

KEVIN SMITH'S GREEN HORNET
VOL. ONE: "SINS OF THE FATHER" & VOL. TWO: "WEARING O' THE GREEN"
written by **KEVIN SMITH**   art by **JONATHAN LAU**   covers by **ALEX ROSS**

Playboy Britt Reid Jr. has lived a frivolous life of luxury. But when a mysterious figure from the past brutally and publicly murders his father, all of that changes. Now, driven by a thirst for vengeance and guided by two generations of Katos, this one time underachiever will find those responsible and take his father's place as Century City's greatest protector – The Green Hornet!

In Stores Now!

 WWW.DYNAMITE.NET • Information • Newsletters • Contests • Downloads • Forums • More

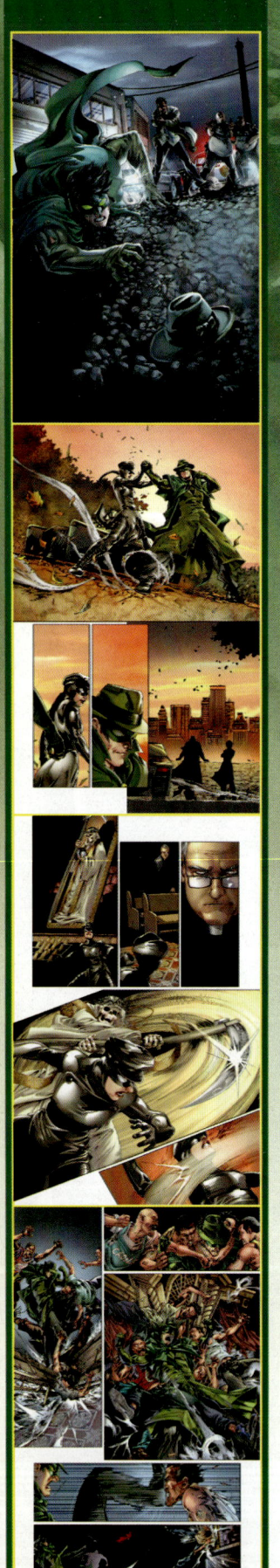